AWESOME FACTS

·FOR·

CURIOUS

KiDS

7

·YEAR OLDS·

Illustrated by
Andrew Pinder

Written by Steve Martin
Edited by Josephine Southon
Designed by Jack Clucas
Cover Design by John Bigwood

With special thanks to
Helen Cumberbatch

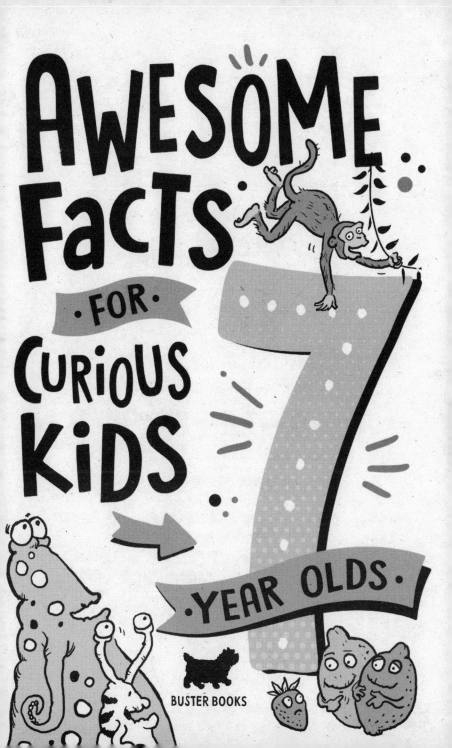

AWESOME FACTS

FOR

CURIOUS KIDS

7 YEAR OLDS

BUSTER BOOKS

First published in Great Britain in 2023 by Buster Books,
an imprint of Michael O'Mara Books Limited,
9 Lion Yard, Tremadoc Road, London SW4 7NQ

W www.mombooks.com/buster

f Buster Books

🐦 @BusterBooks

📷 @buster_books

A CIP catalogue record for this book is available from the British Library.

ISBN: 978-1-78055-926-1

1 3 5 7 9 10 8 6 4 2

This book was printed in February 2023 by
CPI Group (UK) Ltd, Croydon, CR0 4YY.

MIX
Paper | Supporting
responsible forestry
FSC® C171272

CONTENTS

INTRODUCTION

Welcome to this totally
awesome collection of the
coolest facts for curious kids.

In this book you will learn how crocodiles clean
their teeth, why where you live isn't where it
used to be, how police officers see in the dark
and even the best place to see mammoths.
You will also find out all about ...

★ astronaut nappies
(page 76)

★ medieval donkey-kissing
(page 68)

★ cat-sized horses
(page 39)

★ undersea forests
page (43)

★ tomato fights
(page 114)

★ pirate beard-burning
(page 74)

Get ready to dive in and
discover all these incredible
things and more!

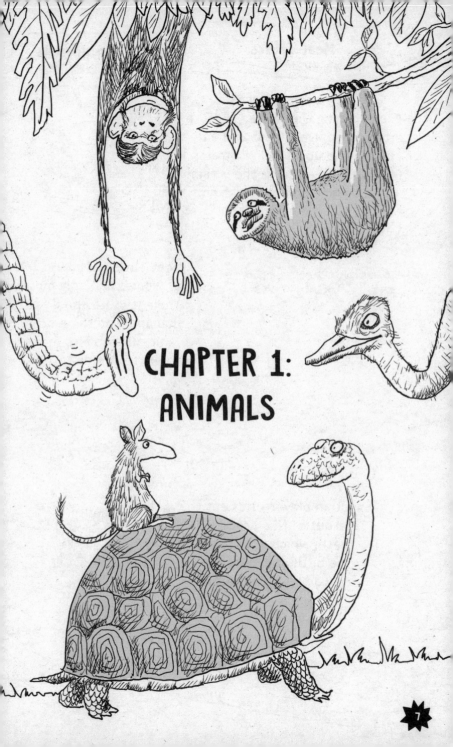

CHAPTER 1:
ANIMALS

Meat-Eaters

Grizzly bears hibernate (sleep during the winter). Before they sleep, they'll eat and eat, putting on up to 180 kilograms (400 pounds) — that's the weight of 8 seven-year-old children.

WHAT? I'M PREPARING FOR HIBERNATION ...

Meat-eating animals such as wolves can only move their jaws up and down. Humans (and some other animals) can also move them from side to side.

Egyptian plover birds eat the food out of Nile crocodiles' teeth, which both feeds the birds and gives the crocodiles clean teeth.

Mongooses won't die from a venomous snake bite. In fact, snakes are a key part of mongooses' diets.

Birds of prey are meat-eating birds. The peregrine falcon can dive on its victim at an unbelievable 320 kilometres (200 miles) per hour.

Not all meat-eaters hunt live animals. Vultures like to eat animals that are already dead.

YOU'RE LUCKY I'M SO KIND. YOU'D NEVER FIND A BIG ENOUGH TOOTHBRUSH!

Pandas love bamboo. It's pretty much all they eat and they can get through 270 kilograms (600 pounds) of it in 1 week — that's about the same weight as 12 seven-year-old children.

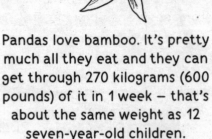

NO NEED TO SHOW OFF, BERNARD ...

Beavers' teeth contain iron, so they are strong enough to chew through tree trunks. They don't eat entire tree trunks, though. They prefer leaves, tree bark and plants.

Some of the largest, strongest mammals are plant-eaters (herbivores). Rhinoceroses and elephants all have a plant-based diet.

Some herbivores have stomachs made up of several parts. Cows, sheep, camels and giraffes swallow their food. Then, they bring it back to their mouth, give it another chew and swallow it into a different part of their stomach.

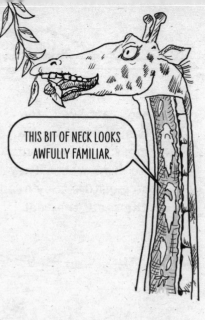

THIS BIT OF NECK LOOKS AWFULLY FAMILIAR.

It's hard for large animals to get all the energy they need just from grass. That's why cows spend up to 12 hours every day eating and then chewing food they have already eaten.

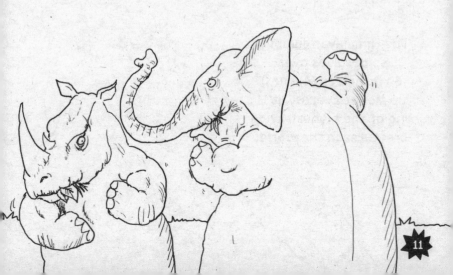

Kangaroo rats live in the deserts of North America. They can survive without having to drink water. They get all the moisture they need from the seeds they eat.

The Alaskan wood frog freezes in the winter. Everything stops, even its heart and its breathing. When the warmer weather arrives, it comes back to life.

The Himalayan jumping spider lives over 6 kilometres (4 miles) up Mount Everest. It is one of the highest-living creatures in the world.

The mighty cockroach can survive without food for a month, and without water for a week. It can hold its breath for 40 minutes and even carry on living without a head.

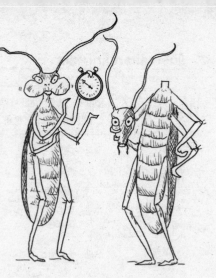

Emperor penguins live in Antarctica where icy winds can reach 200 kilometres (124 miles) per hour. In winter, the male protects an egg for 9 weeks, balancing it on its feet close to its warm body.

BIT CHILLY!

ARE YOU SURE THIS IS THE PLACE?

Some elephants live in the desert. They use their fantastic memories to remember where to find water, and they use their trunks to dig wells.

Australian Animals

THAT WAS A NICE BREAKFAST. RIGHT, TIME FOR BED!

There are 24 hours in a day and koalas sleep for up to 22 of them.

Kangaroos can jump 9 metres (30 feet). That means they could leap over 7 seven-year-old children lying head to toe.

A platypus is a very strange creature. It has a beak (bill) like a duck, a tail like a beaver, and webbed feet with claws. It lays eggs, and shoots poison from its legs.

GULP!

Emus don't behave like most
other birds. They can't fly.
They can run at 50 kilometres
(30 miles) per hour and some are
over 2 metres (6.5 feet) tall.

Redback spiders
like living in houses.
That's bad news for
humans, as their bite
is venomous.

Wombats defend themselves
with their tough bums. When
their burrows are attacked,
they block the entrance
with their bottoms.

The Dog Family

A wolf's howl can be heard from 16 kilometres (10 miles) away.

WOULD YOU MIND NOT MAKING SUCH A MESS?

MAKE YOURSELF USEFUL AND GET CHASING!

The coyote is an American member of the dog family. It often goes hunting with a badger. The coyote does the chasing and the badger does the digging.

Foxes, like some other members of the dog family, are nocturnal (active at night).

Dingoes are wild dogs that live in packs in Australia. They will hunt kangaroos but don't usually bother people.

FEATHERS, IS THAT YOU?

Most jackals live in Africa. They usually talk to each other using a 'yipping' sound, but some jackals hoot like owls.

Huskies were bred to pull sledges across the Arctic snow. They can travel for up to 160 kilometres (100 miles) in a day. It would take a human 8 hours a day for just over 4 days to walk that distance.

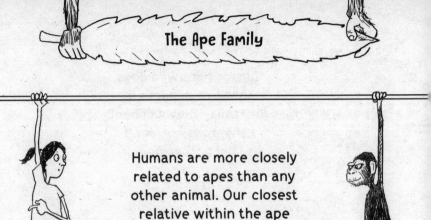

Humans are more closely related to apes than any other animal. Our closest relative within the ape family is the chimpanzee.

Gorillas look fierce, but they are actually plant-eaters and don't hunt other animals.

An orangutan's arms are so long that it can touch its ankles while standing up.

Gibbon families sing together as they travel around the jungle.

YOU KNOW, THESE HUMANS ARE QUITE INTELLIGENT. I THINK SHE UNDERSTOOD WHAT I WAS SAYING.

Bonobos are very intelligent animals. One called Kanzi understood over 300 symbols and used these to 'speak' to a human scientist.

In the River

River otters can hold their breath for up to 4 minutes, closing their ears and nostrils to keep water out.

Beavers build dams across rivers. These dams create deep pools. The beavers build their homes in the pools so dangerous animals can't reach them.

Salmon live at sea but give birth in rivers. They swim incredible distances to the same spot where they were born to lay their eggs.

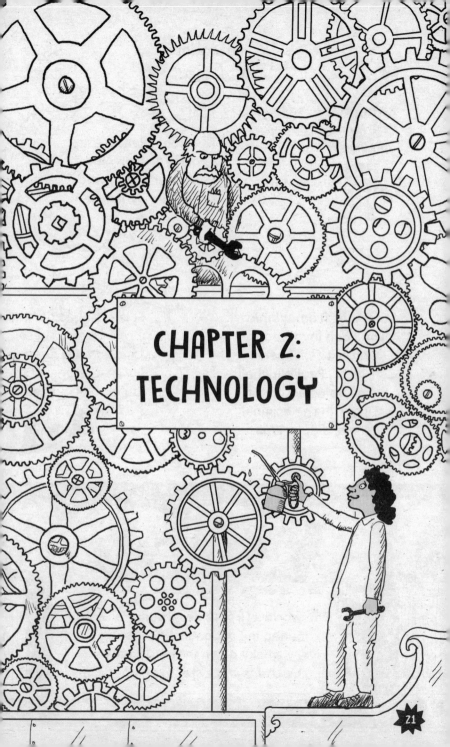

CHAPTER 2: TECHNOLOGY

Inventions

The Nobel Peace Prize is named after Alfred Nobel, the man who invented dynamite.

Tigger from *Winnie the Pooh* invented the first artificial heart. At least, Paul Winchell (the voice actor for Tigger in the original films) did, in 1963.

The world's first underground railway opened in London in 1863. It was very smoky down in the tunnel as the trains were steam engines.

A scientist was working with energy waves called microwaves when the waves melted the chocolate bar in his pocket. This gave him an idea for heating food and he invented the microwave oven.

Tinned food was invented in 1810. The tin opener wasn't invented until the 1850s.

EUREKA!

Archimedes, an inventor in ancient Greece, had a brilliant idea while he was in the bath. He was so excited that he ran down the street shouting "Eureka!" (which means "I've found it!"). Unfortunately, he forgot to put his clothes on first.

The internet and the World Wide Web aren't the same. The internet is a huge number of computers linked together. The World Wide Web is all the web pages on these computers.

Development of the internet began in the 1960s, but the first web page wasn't created until 1991.

The first email was sent in 1971. The British Queen sent her first email 5 years later. The first spam (unwanted) email was sent 2 years after that.

There are different ways to search for web pages. Most people use Google, which makes over 60,000 searches every second.

It's not just computers, phones and tablets that are connected to the internet. Spectacles, egg cartons, toothbrushes and even rubbish bins have been linked to the internet using electronic sensors.

Jet packs are real! They aren't seen very often because they are very expensive, so it might be a long time before children use them to travel to school.

Japan is famous for its speedy trains. The fastest travels at 602 kilometres (374 miles) per hour. That's over 5 times faster than a car speeding along a motorway.

Submarines have large water tanks. They sink by filling up the tanks with water and then rise by letting the water out.

ThrustSSC was the first car
to go faster than the speed
of sound. At 1,228 kilometres
(763 miles) per hour, it travelled
faster than a passenger aircraft.

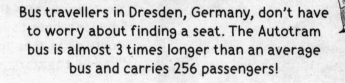

Bus travellers in Dresden, Germany, don't have
to worry about finding a seat. The Autotram
bus is almost 3 times longer than an average
bus and carries 256 passengers!

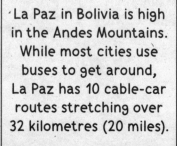

La Paz in Bolivia is high
in the Andes Mountains.
While most cities use
buses to get around,
La Paz has 10 cable-car
routes stretching over
32 kilometres (20 miles).

X-rays let doctors see bones inside bodies. The 'X' means 'unknown' because a professor discovered the rays by accident and didn't know what they were at the time.

There are telescopes in space. They are put there because they can see more clearly and they don't have to wait until night-time to view the stars.

Modern microscopes can make tiny objects look up to 50 million times bigger.

There is a camera that is so tiny that doctors can inject it into the patient's body through a needle. They can then take pictures to learn about the patient's health.

Police helicopters can find people hiding in a dark forest in the middle of the night. Thermal imaging cameras detect heat from people's bodies to make an image.

Night-vision goggles take a low light and make it larger so we can see in the dark. They turn things green as it is easier for people to see this colour against a dark background.

Robots

The Sam100 bricklayer robot can lay 3,000 bricks a day. A human bricklayer lays about 500 a day.

Industrial robots carry out work for us. The first one was created in 1937 and was made out of a children's toy.

Cassie the robot can complete a 5-kilometre (3-mile) run. Another robot, OutRunner, can run at 32 kilometres (20 miles) per hour.

HEY, SLOW DOWN!

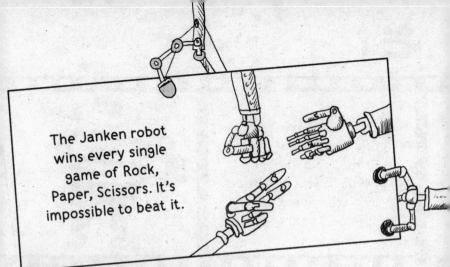

The Janken robot wins every single game of Rock, Paper, Scissors. It's impossible to beat it.

There are robots that can play musical instruments, including the drums, piano and bass guitar.

WHO'S HE?

A filmmaker made a programme about crabs by creating a robot spy crab fitted with a camera. The crab travelled around with the real crabs and filmed some amazing scenes.

The first movie that told a story was *The Great Train Robbery* in 1903. It was inspired by a true event that happened 3 years before.

Before computers, cartoons needed 24 different drawings for every second of film. That meant drawing 86,400 pictures for an hour of film.

Animated films now use computers to make the images. This is called computer-generated imagery (CGI). The first-ever full-length CGI movie was *Toy Story*.

CHAPTER 3:
PREHISTORIC WORLD

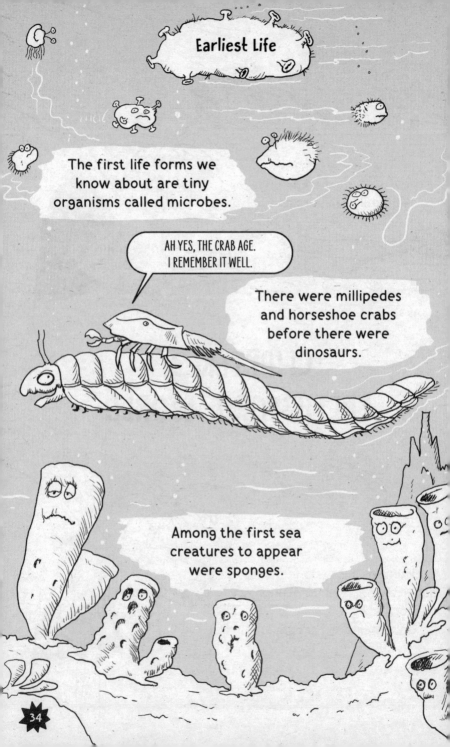

Earliest Life

The first life forms we know about are tiny organisms called microbes.

AH YES, THE CRAB AGE. I REMEMBER IT WELL.

There were millipedes and horseshoe crabs before there were dinosaurs.

Among the first sea creatures to appear were sponges.

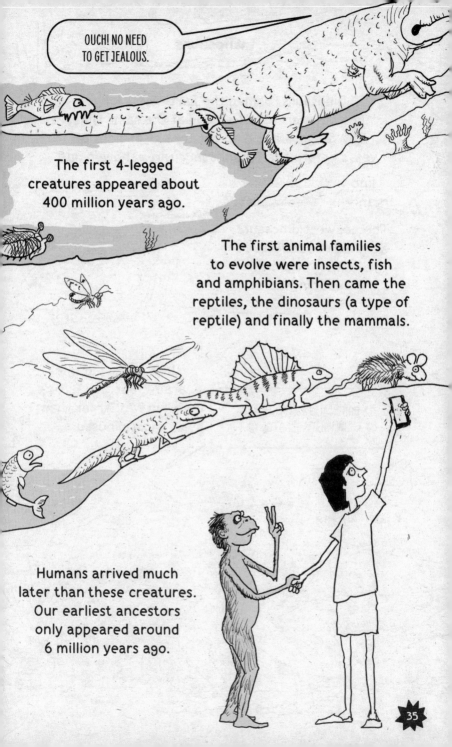

OUCH! NO NEED TO GET JEALOUS.

The first 4-legged creatures appeared about 400 million years ago.

The first animal families to evolve were insects, fish and amphibians. Then came the reptiles, the dinosaurs (a type of reptile) and finally the mammals.

Humans arrived much later than these creatures. Our earliest ancestors only appeared around 6 million years ago.

Dinosaurs

Dinosaurs roamed the Earth for a long time but weren't all around at the same time. The *Stegosaurus* died out tens of millions of years before the *Tyrannosaurus rex* showed up.

The heaviest dinosaurs weighed about 100,000 times more than the lightest dinosaurs.

Dinosaurs had small brains, but the *T. rex*'s brain was larger than most dinosaurs.

DON'T CALL ME STUPID IF YOU KNOW WHAT'S GOOD FOR YOU!

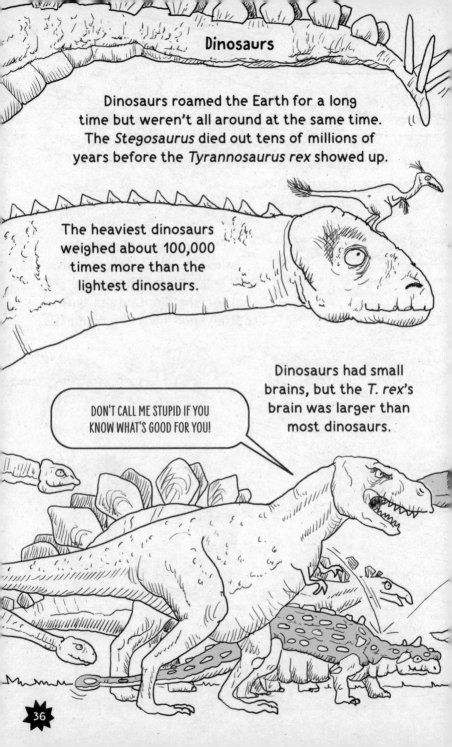

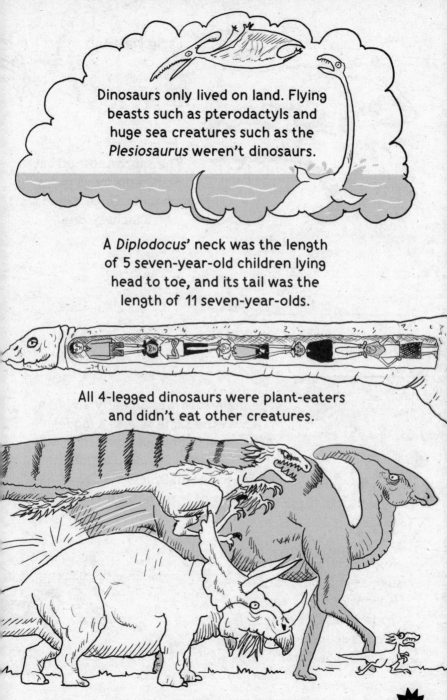

Dinosaurs only lived on land. Flying beasts such as pterodactyls and huge sea creatures such as the *Plesiosaurus* weren't dinosaurs.

A *Diplodocus'* neck was the length of 5 seven-year-old children lying head to toe, and its tail was the length of 11 seven-year-olds.

All 4-legged dinosaurs were plant-eaters and didn't eat other creatures.

Early Mammals

The sabre-toothed cat had 2 enormous fangs, each up to 20 centimetres (8 inches) long.

CAN'T YOU DRAW SOMETHING ELSE? I'M SICK OF LOOKING AT MAMMOTHS.

The mammoth was an early elephant. It was the same size as a modern African elephant but covered in hair. The Cave of a Hundred Mammoths in France actually has 158 Stone Age pictures of mammoths on its walls.

Rodents are animals such as mice and rats. Millions of years ago, rodents as heavy as cows scampered across the Earth.

The largest-ever land mammal was a bit like a huge, hornless rhinoceros. The main difference was that it was over 3 times taller than a black rhino, more than twice as long and 15 times heavier.

The entelodon was an enormous, terrifying pig. It was as big as a bison and had a very mean temper.

Not everything was big in prehistoric times. About 50 million years ago, horse-like creatures the size of large cats galloped across the land.

GOOD PUSS.

The Stone Age

Our ancestors first started using stone tools over 3 million years ago. Then, about 5,000 years ago, humans began to use metal.

Stone tools included hammers, axes and spear points.

One of the world's oldest pieces of art, a small sculpture of a woman, was found in a cave in Germany. It's up to 40,000 years old.

I WARNED YOU NOT TO MAKE SO MUCH FURNITURE.

One reason that Stone Age people lived in caves is because they were nomads. This means they didn't live in one place but moved around, following animal herds.

It's amazing what people find in caves. In 2008, a 35,000-year-old flute was discovered. It was made out of a vulture bone.

Until 40,000 years ago, another species (type) of human existed. They were called Neanderthals. They were like us but shorter, more muscular and their faces stuck out more than ours.

Land masses move around. Millions of years ago, they were nearly all joined together. Now, there are seas and oceans between land masses, such as Europe and North America.

About 18,000 years ago, ice sheets over 3.5 kilometres (2 miles) thick covered a lot of the planet. This period of time was called the Ice Age.

Scientists think the first humans appeared in Africa.

Americans love visiting Yellowstone Park. However, about 640,000 years ago it made a bigger volcanic explosion than any human has ever seen.

Millions of years ago, crocodiles lived in the Arctic. Of course, it was much warmer then than it is now.

IT'S LOVELY HERE! I HOPE I DON'T GET SUNBURNT, THOUGH.

Divers have found the remains of forests under the sea. This is because sea levels change and what is now sea used to be land.

Fossils

Fossils are the remains of creatures preserved in rock and are usually millions of years old. They can be tiny insects or huge dinosaurs.

In the past, people who found dinosaur bones thought they belonged to dragons or giants.

Fossils of ancient sea creatures have been found on the world's tallest mountain, Mount Everest. Before the land was pushed up, Everest must have been under the sea.

Amber is a beautiful gemstone that was a liquid (tree resin) millions of years ago. Sometimes, insects from prehistoric times can be seen trapped inside pieces of it.

The fossil of an ancient whale was found in the Sahara Desert. This might seem like an odd place to find a whale, but millions of years ago the Sahara was under the sea.

I GUESS WE'LL NEVER KNOW WHO WOULD HAVE WON.

One of the most awesome fossils ever found was of 2 dinosaurs fighting. A *Velociraptor* and a *Protoceratops* were clawing and biting each other.

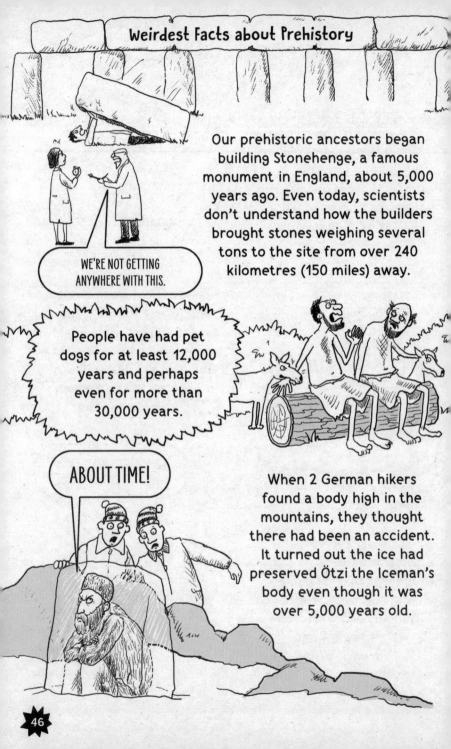

WE'RE NOT GETTING ANYWHERE WITH THIS.

Our prehistoric ancestors began building Stonehenge, a famous monument in England, about 5,000 years ago. Even today, scientists don't understand how the builders brought stones weighing several tons to the site from over 240 kilometres (150 miles) away.

People have had pet dogs for at least 12,000 years and perhaps even for more than 30,000 years.

ABOUT TIME!

When 2 German hikers found a body high in the mountains, they thought there had been an accident. It turned out the ice had preserved Ötzi the Iceman's body even though it was over 5,000 years old.

CHAPTER 4:
PLANET EARTH

Wild Weather

A blizzard is a mix of snow and wind. A blizzard in Iran lasted for 6 days and produced 8 metres (26 feet) of snow. That's enough to cover a 2-storey house.

A hailstone as big as a soccer ball thumped to the ground in America during a storm. It was 20 centimetres (8 inches) wide.

Avalanches can cause snow to rush down a mountain at more than 320 kilometres (200 miles) per hour.

Tsunamis are huge waves that can be over 30 metres (100 feet) tall. That's high enough to reach the top of a 10-storey building.

Some of Japan's roads have underground heating to melt snow so that cars can still travel safely in winter.

49

Amazing Africa!

The continent of Africa has 54 countries. The largest is Algeria. The country with the most people is Nigeria.

Africa's Victoria Falls aren't the tallest in the world, but they are the biggest. They are over 100 metres (over 350 feet) high and more than 1.5 kilometres (over a mile) wide.

DON'T WORRY! I'M DORMANT!

Mount Kilimanjaro, Africa's tallest mountain, is actually a volcano. Luckily, the huge mountain hasn't had a major eruption for 360,000 years.

Africa has lots of large animals that are found nowhere else in the wild. These include zebras, hippopotamuses, giraffes, gorillas, wildebeest, and black rhinoceroses.

The Sahara Desert covers about a quarter of Africa and the huge grasslands called the Savanna cover about half of the continent.

JAMBO!

SELAM!

Over 2,000 languages are spoken in Africa.

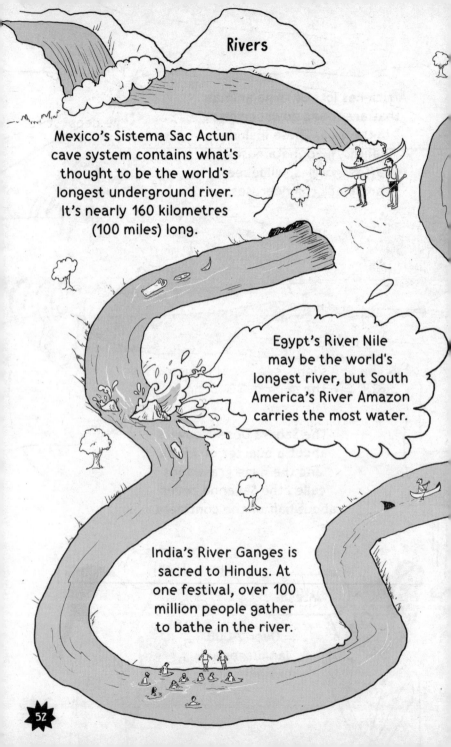

Rivers

Mexico's Sistema Sac Actun cave system contains what's thought to be the world's longest underground river. It's nearly 160 kilometres (100 miles) long.

Egypt's River Nile may be the world's longest river, but South America's River Amazon carries the most water.

India's River Ganges is sacred to Hindus. At one festival, over 100 million people gather to bathe in the river.

OI! WHO'S BEEN THROWING ALL THESE TOWERS IN THE RIVER?

Africa's River Congo is the deepest river in the world. It is 220 metres (720 feet) deep in places. If you stood the Leaning Tower of Pisa on top of Big Ben, the river would still cover them.

The USA's longest river, the Missouri, flows into the country's second-longest river, the Mississippi. Each river is over 3,750 kilometres (2,300 miles) long.

Although the Yangtze River is 6,300 kilometres (3,915 miles) long, it never leaves China.

Mountains

About 750 people try to climb
the world's highest mountain,
Mount Everest, every year.
About 500 make it to the top.

Climbing and
descending Everest
is the equivalent to
climbing up and down
58,070 stairs.

La Paz, the capital of Bolivia,
is in the Andes Mountains.
When you get off the
plane at the airport, you
are still over 4 kilometres
(2.5 miles) above sea level.

The Himalayas can be found
north-east of India, and
9 out of the 10 highest
mountains in the world
are found there.

Don't climb Mount Fuji if you
want to be by yourself. Although
the climbing season only lasts for
2 months of the year, 400,000
people climb to the top every year.

There's a railway tunnel running underneath
the Alps in Switzerland that's 57 kilometres
(35 miles) long. It took 17 years to build
and is over 2 kilometres (nearly 1.5 miles)
deep below the mountains.

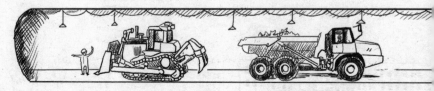

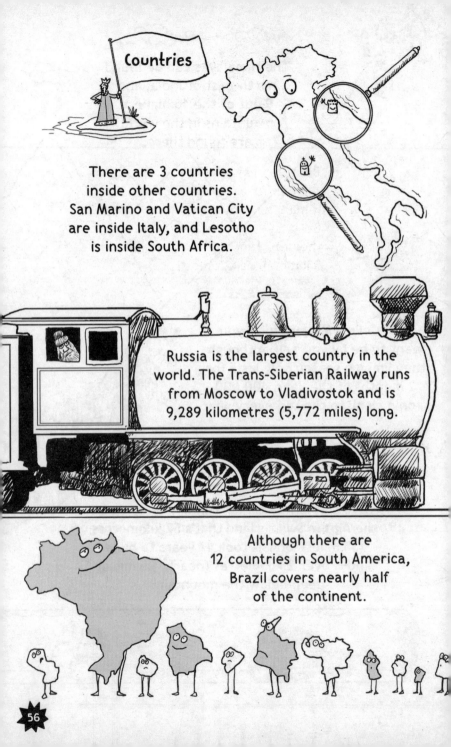

Countries

There are 3 countries inside other countries. San Marino and Vatican City are inside Italy, and Lesotho is inside South Africa.

Russia is the largest country in the world. The Trans-Siberian Railway runs from Moscow to Vladivostok and is 9,289 kilometres (5,772 miles) long.

Although there are 12 countries in South America, Brazil covers nearly half of the continent.

Bhutan and Nepal are 2 countries in the Himalayan mountains. Both have an average height of more than 3 kilometres (2 miles).

Chile is very skinny, with an average width of only 177 kilometres (110 miles) and a height of about 4,300 kilometres (2,670 miles).

Norway has 5 villages called Å. Wales has a village called Llanfairpwllgwyngyllgogerychwyrndrobwllllantysiliogogogoch.

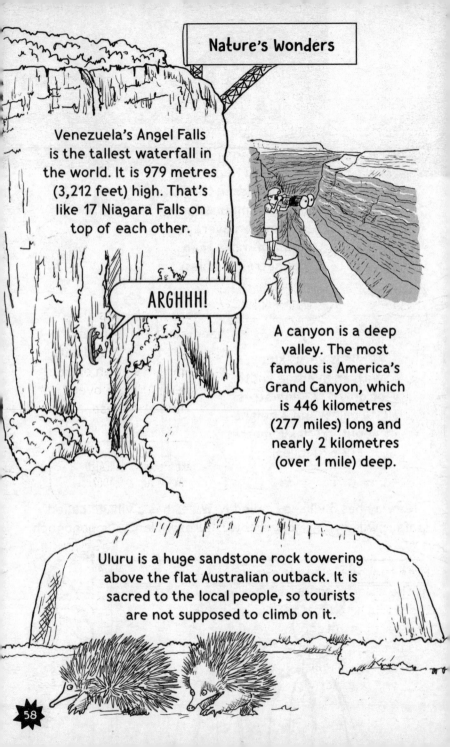

Nature's Wonders

Venezuela's Angel Falls is the tallest waterfall in the world. It is 979 metres (3,212 feet) high. That's like 17 Niagara Falls on top of each other.

ARGHHH!

A canyon is a deep valley. The most famous is America's Grand Canyon, which is 446 kilometres (277 miles) long and nearly 2 kilometres (over 1 mile) deep.

Uluru is a huge sandstone rock towering above the flat Australian outback. It is sacred to the local people, so tourists are not supposed to climb on it.

In the far north, the dark, night sky can light up with beautiful dancing green and blue lights. This amazing display is called the Northern Lights.

HOW DID YOU GET OVER THERE?

Norway's fjords are spectacular valleys where the sea travels inland with steep mountains on either side. There are over 1,000 of these.

ARE THE BUBBLES CREATED BY THE VOLCANO, TOO?

Even though Iceland is one of the coldest countries in the world, the local people love bathing outdoors. This is because the water is warmed by underground volcanic activity.

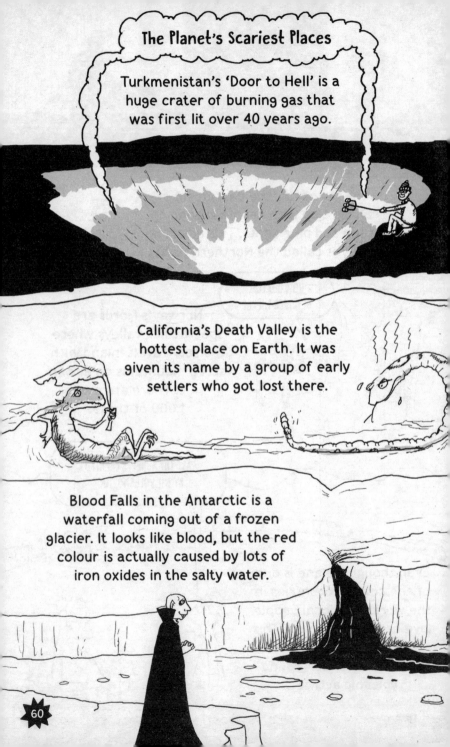

The Planet's Scariest Places

Turkmenistan's 'Door to Hell' is a huge crater of burning gas that was first lit over 40 years ago.

California's Death Valley is the hottest place on Earth. It was given its name by a group of early settlers who got lost there.

Blood Falls in the Antarctic is a waterfall coming out of a frozen glacier. It looks like blood, but the red colour is actually caused by lots of iron oxides in the salty water.

CHAPTER 5:
HISTORY

Famous People

The British king, Henry the 8th (written Henry VIII), ruled in the 16th century and was famous for having 6 wives. He had 2 of them beheaded.

Helen Keller was a world-famous writer, educator and campaigner who was nominated for a Nobel Prize. Being blind and deaf from the age of 1 certainly didn't stop her achieving great things.

Leonardo da Vinci created a design for a helicopter. That might not sound very impressive until you learn that he drew it in the 15th century. That's over 400 years before helicopters were invented.

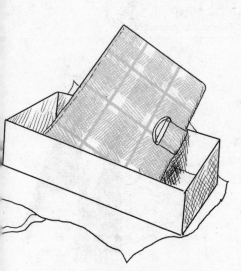

When Anne Frank was given a diary for her 13th birthday, no one knew it would become a famous book. The young Jewish girl wrote about her time hiding from the Nazis in the early 1940s.

Confucius is the most famous teacher of all time. Even though he lived 2,500 years ago, people still study this Chinese thinker's lessons.

Isaac Newton was a great scientist. He is believed to have got his best idea — about why things fall to Earth — when an apple fell on his head as he sat in the garden.

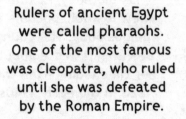

Rulers of ancient Egypt were called pharaohs. One of the most famous was Cleopatra, who ruled until she was defeated by the Roman Empire.

In 1922, the lost tomb of the pharaoh Tutankhamun was discovered. It was full of incredible treasure. His body was found in a solid gold coffin and wearing a beautiful golden mask.

Ancient Egyptians turned bodies into mummies. One job was using a hook to pull the brain out. through the nose.

The Great Pyramid of Giza is the largest Egyptian pyramid. It has over 2.3 million stones, many of which were heavier than a hippopotamus.

The Egyptians wrote using pictures called hieroglyphs. There were over 1,000 of these.

Cats were so important to the ancient Egyptians that there are even cat mummies!

Ancient Rome

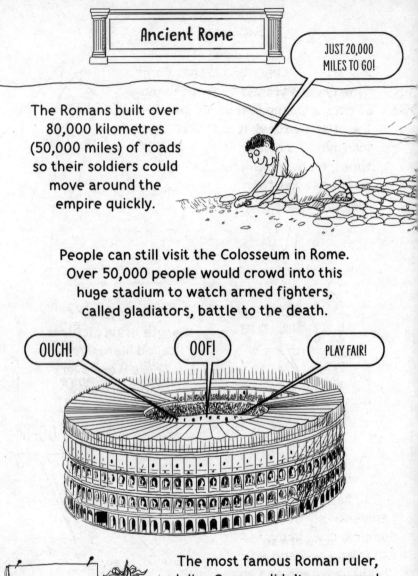

The Romans built over 80,000 kilometres (50,000 miles) of roads so their soldiers could move around the empire quickly.

JUST 20,000 MILES TO GO!

People can still visit the Colosseum in Rome. Over 50,000 people would crowd into this huge stadium to watch armed fighters, called gladiators, battle to the death.

OUCH!

OOF!

PLAY FAIR!

The most famous Roman ruler, Julius Caesar, didn't pay enough attention when he was warned to "Beware the Ides [the 15th] of March". That was the day he was killed by his enemies.

Legend says that Rome was built by twins Romulus and Remus. As children, they were looked after and fed by a wolf.

Ancient Rome lasted over 1,000 years. It began as a sleepy, little village and grew to become a huge, powerful empire.

IT'S NOT LIKE IT WAS IN THE OLD DAYS.

You can still visit the ancient Roman town of Pompeii. It was covered in ash from a volcano nearly 2,000 years ago and lost for hundreds of years.

OOPS!

Sick and Stinky

The Great Plague killed thousands of people in the 17th century. One cure people tried was to store farts in jars and let them out when the plague was around.

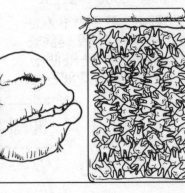

In the Middle Ages, if people needed a tooth pulled out they'd go to the barber. For toothache, some people believed the cure was to kiss a donkey.

For hundreds of years, doctors stuck blood-drinking worms, called leeches, on a diseased person's skin to suck their blood.

SILK OR GOOSE DOWN TODAY, SIRE?

The Groom of the Stool had various important roles in 16th-century England. One of them, it is said, involved wiping the king's bum!

In ancient Greece, people bought bottles of athletes' sweat to rub on themselves. They believed it cured aches and pains.

THIS BATHING BUSINESS SEEMS A HUGE WASTE OF TIME ...

Queen Isabella of Spain lived in the 15th century. She boasted that she only had 2 baths in her whole life – once when she was born and once when she was getting married.

In 1429, 17-year-old Joan of Arc led the French to a famous victory over the English. The English were so annoyed that they had her burned at the stake in 1431.

Mahatma Gandhi led India to freedom from British rule. He became famous for refusing to use any violence to defeat the enemy.

In 1955, Rosa Parks wouldn't give her bus seat to a white man and was arrested. She became known as the mother of the campaign for equal rights for black people in America.

Florence Nightingale invented modern nursing while looking after wounded soldiers during a 19th-century war. She was called 'The Lady with the Lamp' because she would work through the night.

In the First World War, a pigeon messenger raced to help some trapped soldiers. He was shot in the chest and leg, and blinded in 1 eye. He kept going, saved the soldiers and was awarded a medal. What a brave little pigeon!

Warriors

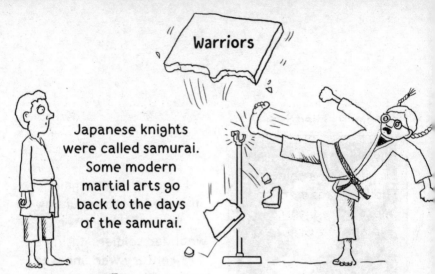

Japanese knights were called samurai. Some modern martial arts go back to the days of the samurai.

Medieval knights started their training at 7 years old. They spent 7 years as a page, another 7 years as a squire and then became a knight.

Over 2,000 years ago, the first Chinese emperor was buried with thousands of statues. There were 7,000 life-size soldiers, 600 horses and 100 chariots. They can still be visited today.

In a place called Sparta, every 7-year-old boy had to leave home and start training as a soldier. The Spartans were the most feared warriors in ancient Greece.

Boudicca was a Celtic warrior queen who led her fierce followers in battle against the Romans. They destroyed 3 Roman towns and killed tens of thousands of Romans before being stopped.

Led by Genghis Khan, the Mongols travelled from their home in Mongolia and conquered huge areas of Asia and China. The Mongol Empire was the largest land empire of all time.

Pirate captain Blackbeard made himself look extra scary by putting bits of candle in his beard. Then, he charged into battle with smoke pouring from it!

In the Second World War, many British troops were trapped at the French port of Dunkirk. Over 800 ships, yachts, ferries, lifeboats and fishing trawlers set sail to rescue over 330,000 soldiers.

NICE TO FINALLY MEET YOU!

Measuring 193 kilometres (120 miles) long, the Suez Canal was built in Egypt in the 19th century to join the Mediterranean Sea to the Red Sea. This hugely reduced the journey from Europe to Asia.

CHAPTER 6:
SPACE

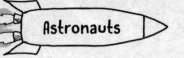

Astronauts

Astronauts wear nappies under their spacesuits. They call them 'Maximum Absorbency Garments', which sounds much more grown up.

Because people float in space (an experience called 'weightlessness'), their muscles don't need to work hard and they shrink. That's why astronauts in space exercise for over 2 hours every day.

Astronauts weigh nothing when floating around in space, but spacesuits actually weigh 127 kilograms (280 pounds). That's more than the weight of 5 seven-year-old children.

Astronauts train in an aeroplane that dives down to cause weightlessness. It makes the trainees feel so ill, the plane's nickname is the 'Vomit Comet'.

It takes 45 minutes to put on a spacesuit and then another hour to get used to it. That's almost 2 hours just to get ready for work.

Out of every 12,000 people who apply to be an astronaut, only 10 will be successful.

Space and the Senses

I CAN'T HEAR YOU!

There is no sound in space, so it's no good shouting for help. This is because there are not enough particles in space for sound waves to travel on.

Astronauts say that space smells of metal.

DO YOU SMELL METAL?

Astronauts like spicy food because being in space weakens their sense of taste.

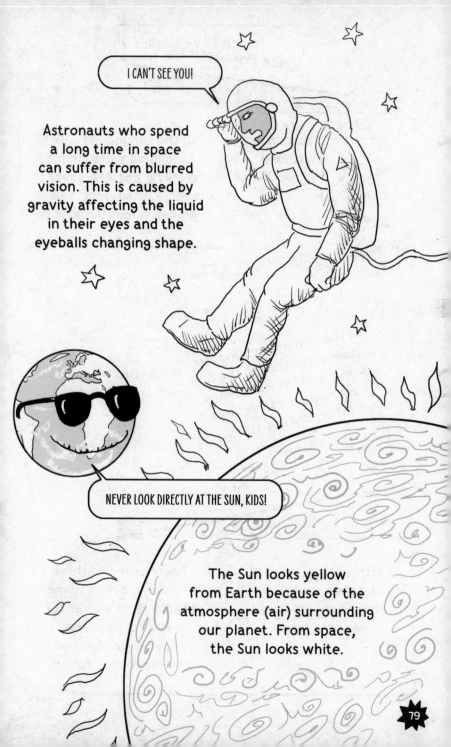

I CAN'T SEE YOU!

Astronauts who spend a long time in space can suffer from blurred vision. This is caused by gravity affecting the liquid in their eyes and the eyeballs changing shape.

NEVER LOOK DIRECTLY AT THE SUN, KIDS!

The Sun looks yellow from Earth because of the atmosphere (air) surrounding our planet. From space, the Sun looks white.

Space Discoveries

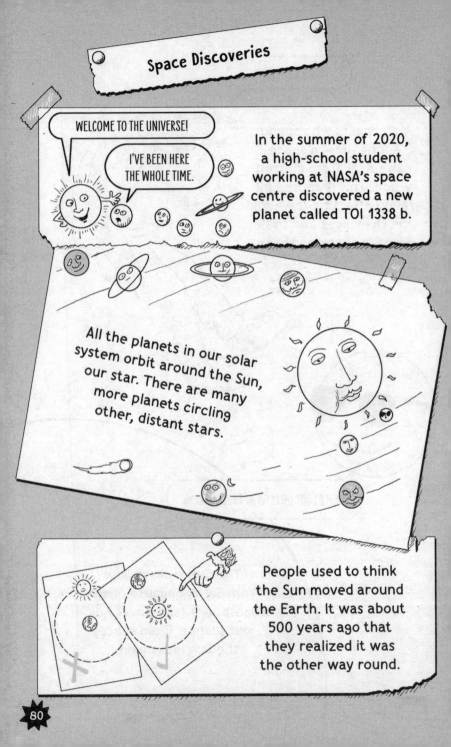

WELCOME TO THE UNIVERSE!

I'VE BEEN HERE THE WHOLE TIME.

In the summer of 2020, a high-school student working at NASA's space centre discovered a new planet called TOI 1338 b.

All the planets in our solar system orbit around the Sun, our star. There are many more planets circling other, distant stars.

People used to think the Sun moved around the Earth. It was about 500 years ago that they realized it was the other way round.

Telescopes weren't much good until a man called Galileo improved them about 400 years ago. When he pointed his telescope at the night sky, he was the first person to see the rings around Saturn.

When a new planet was discovered in our solar system in 1930, 11-year-old Venetia Burney came up with the name Pluto. That's what it's been called ever since.

In 2011, a 10-year-old girl discovered an exploding star in the night sky.

I DIDN'T DO IT, HONEST! IT WAS ALREADY EXPLODING WHEN I FOUND IT.

Satellites

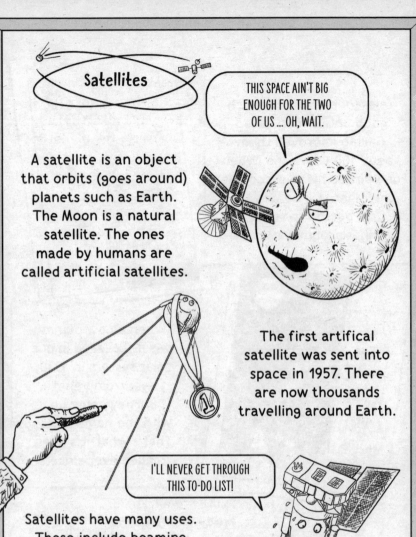

THIS SPACE AIN'T BIG ENOUGH FOR THE TWO OF US ... OH, WAIT.

A satellite is an object that orbits (goes around) planets such as Earth. The Moon is a natural satellite. The ones made by humans are called artificial satellites.

The first artifical satellite was sent into space in 1957. There are now thousands travelling around Earth.

I'LL NEVER GET THROUGH THIS TO-DO LIST!

Satellites have many uses. These include beaming programmes to our TVs, sending messages across the world, guiding car drivers on their journeys and helping to forecast the weather.

Scientists send satellites that no longer work further away from Earth. They will circle the planet in a 'graveyard orbit' for a long, long time.

Satellites reach space by hitching a ride on a rocket. Once the rocket reaches the right place, it releases the satellite.

Asteroids, Comets and Meteors

An asteroid is a rocky object that orbits the Sun. Some are huge, others are as small as pebbles.

There are millions of asteroids travelling around the Sun between Mars and Jupiter. This area is called the asteroid belt.

A comet is a lump of ice, rock and dust that flies around in space. It has a long tail made of dust and gas.

The most famous comet is called Halley's Comet. It flies past Earth once every 75 to 76 years. Its next visit will be in 2061.

A meteor is a rocky object that enters the Earth's atmosphere (the air) and burns up, creating a flash of light in the sky.

Two billion years ago, a huge meteor crashed into Earth, leaving a crater of up to 300 kilometres (185 miles) wide. Part of the crater is still there, in Africa.

Rockets and Rovers

The Saturn V ('5')
rocket needed almost
2 million litres (over 520,000
gallons) of fuel for take-off.
A car could drive over
32.5 million kilometres
(20 million miles) on
that amount.

The first space
tourist took off in a
Russian Soyuz rocket
in 2001. American
Dennis Tito spent
$20 million to travel
to the International
Space Station for a
week's holiday.

Apollo 11 was the
first mission to land
humans on the Moon.
The rocket that took the
astronauts there is one
of the largest and
strongest ever built.

Mars Curiosity rover is an unpiloted vehicle exploring Mars. It took 10 years to drive nearly 29 kilometres (18 miles) across the surface.

CURIOSITY ROVER, REPORTING FOR DUTY!

Professor Sanjeev Gupta sat in his London flat, above a hair salon, controlling another Mars rover named Perseverance. It was about 225 million kilometres (140 million miles) away.

The Voyager 1 space probe was launched in 1977 and has now left our solar system. It moves over 16 kilometres (10 miles) further into interstellar space every second.

Space Talk

DON'T PANIC

"Okay Houston, we've had a problem here!" was the message sent to Mission Control in Texas by Apollo 13 after an explosion, over 320,000 kilometres (200,000 miles) from Earth. The astronauts made it home safely.

When Neil Armstrong became the first person to set foot on the Moon, he said, "That's one small step for man, one giant leap for mankind."

WHAT ABOUT ALIENKIND?

The first thing that Charles Conrad said when he stepped on to the Moon was **"Whoopee!"**

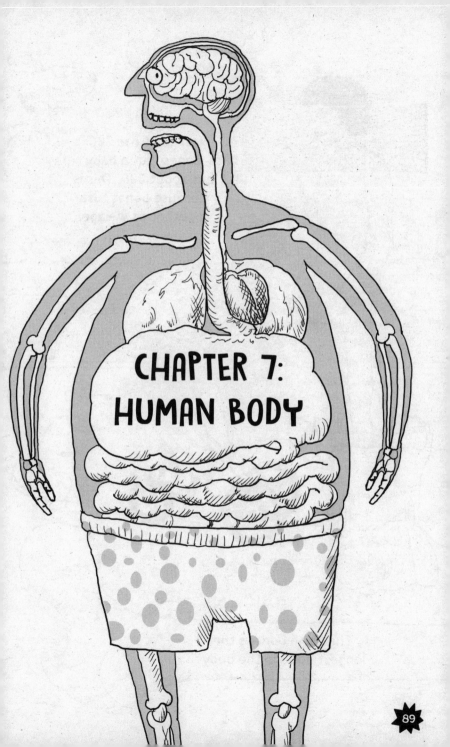

CHAPTER 7:
HUMAN BODY

Bones

An adult has 206 bones, but a baby has about 300. This is because bones fuse together as we age.

The thigh bone is the longest bone in the body.

Out of the 206 bones in an adult's body, the feet contain 52 of them.

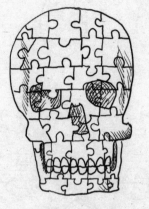

The skull is made from 22 different bones joined together.

Teeth are the only part of the human body that can't fully repair themselves.

Joints are where 2 bones meet, such as the knee and the elbow. There are 360 joints in an adult's body.

NICE TO MEET YOU ... AGAIN.

Eyes

Your eyebrows might seem pointless but they have 2 important jobs. They protect your eyes from sweat and rain, and they help you show feelings.

We see with our brains, not our eyes. Our brains make sense of the signals sent to them by our eyes.

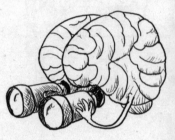

Your eye is 6 times larger than the part you can see when you look in the mirror.

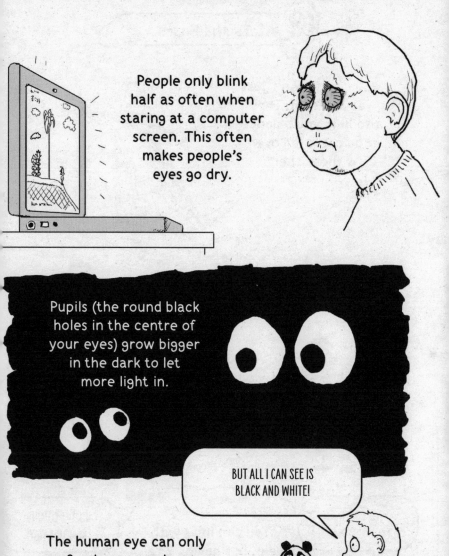

People only blink half as often when staring at a computer screen. This often makes people's eyes go dry.

Pupils (the round black holes in the centre of your eyes) grow bigger in the dark to let more light in.

BUT ALL I CAN SEE IS BLACK AND WHITE!

The human eye can only see 3 colours — red, green and blue. All other colours we see are a mix of these 3 colours.

Ears and Noses

Your ears aren't just for listening. They also help you balance. You could fall over without them.

Children can hear sounds that adults can't. Adults can't hear high-pitched whistles.

You can hear with 1 ear, but having 2 tells you where the sound is coming from.

IT'S COMING FROM THIS WAY!

NO, IT'S COMING FROM THIS WAY!

Smell is important when it comes to tasting food. If someone eats while pinching their nose, the flavour is very different.

When breathing in, your nose cleans the air before it goes down to your lungs.

Your nose is also a heater. When you breathe in, it warms the air until it reaches body temperature.

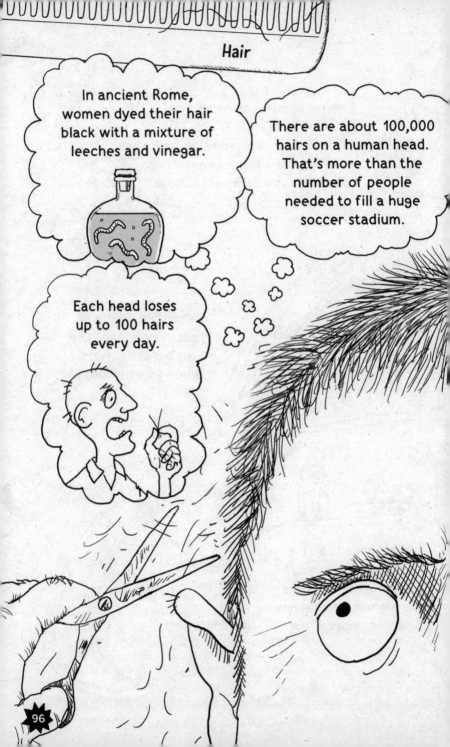

In ancient Rome, women dyed their hair black with a mixture of leeches and vinegar.

There are about 100,000 hairs on a human head. That's more than the number of people needed to fill a huge soccer stadium.

Each head loses up to 100 hairs every day.

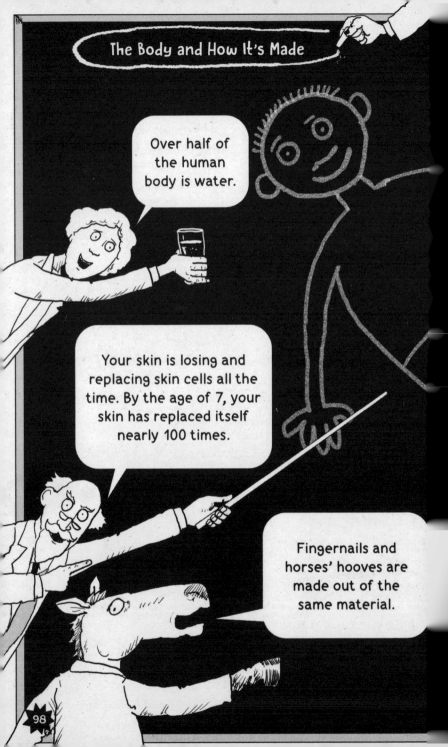

Bodies are made out of dust that came from the stars!

Your bones grow new cells and gradually replace themselves every 10 years. If you are 7 years old now, in 3 years you will have a completely different skeleton from the one you were born with.

Some body parts don't do much. Our appendix is an organ that seems to do nothing at all.

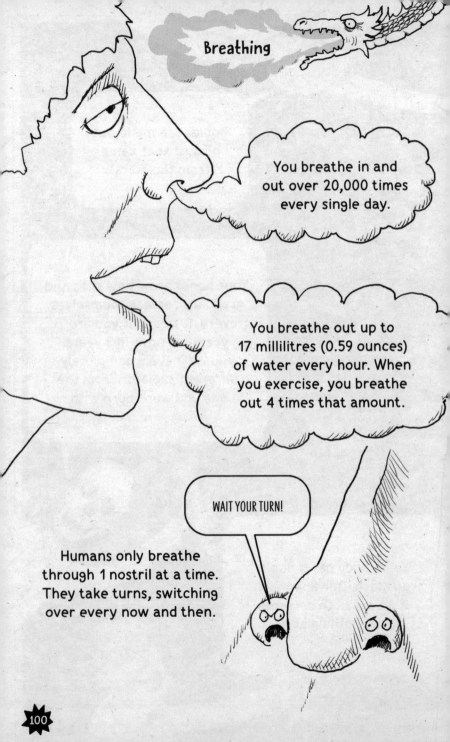

Breathing

You breathe in and out over 20,000 times every single day.

You breathe out up to 17 millilitres (0.59 ounces) of water every hour. When you exercise, you breathe out 4 times that amount.

WAIT YOUR TURN!

Humans only breathe through 1 nostril at a time. They take turns, switching over every now and then.

Your lungs have around 300 million tiny bags inside, each one holding a tiny amount of air.

You have 2 lungs, 1 on either side of your chest. The one on your left side is smaller because it needs to make room for the heart.

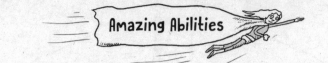

Marathon races of just over 26 miles (42 kilometres) are too tough for most people, but in China in 2004, Xu Zhenjun ran the whole race backwards.

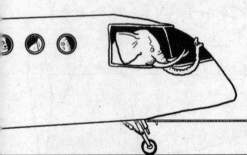

A Canadian man pulled a plane weighing 189 tonnes (over 416,000 pounds). That's about the same as 35 full-grown elephants.

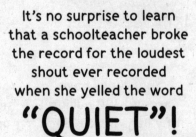

It's no surprise to learn that a schoolteacher broke the record for the loudest shout ever recorded when she yelled the word

"QUIET"!

CHAPTER 8: FOOD

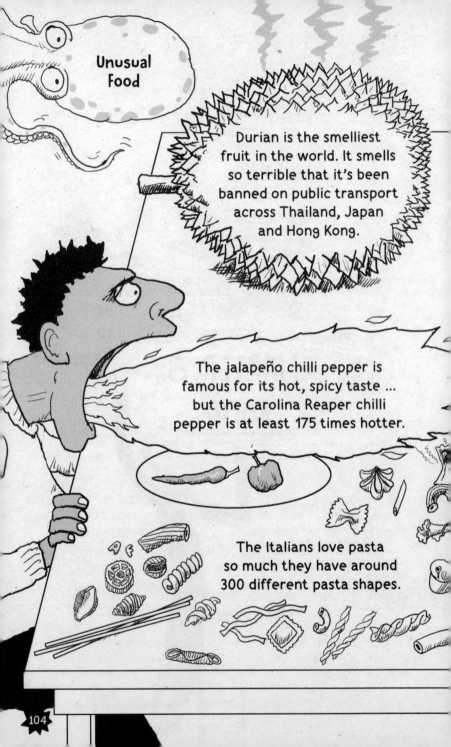

Unusual Food

Durian is the smelliest fruit in the world. It smells so terrible that it's been banned on public transport across Thailand, Japan and Hong Kong.

The jalapeño chilli pepper is famous for its hot, spicy taste ... but the Carolina Reaper chilli pepper is at least 175 times hotter.

The Italians love pasta so much they have around 300 different pasta shapes.

Making model gingerbread houses is popular at Christmas. In Texas, a full-size one was built using 3,266 kilograms (7,200 pounds) of flour, 7,200 eggs and 1,361 kilograms (3,000 pounds) of sugar.

Chefs sometimes add gold to food. Gold might be very valuable but it has no flavour at all.

An American company made a chocolate chip cookie that was as wide as 25 seven-year-olds lying head to toe. It weighed more than 1.5 million normal cookies.

One of the most harvested food crops in the world is wheat. Over 680 million tonnes (750 million tons) of wheat was produced in 2019 alone. That's almost 75,000 times the weight of the Eiffel Tower.

China grows over one-third of the world's peanuts. We need a lot of them as it takes over 500 peanuts to make a single jar of peanut butter.

Rice is grown underwater to keep pests and weeds away (pests and weeds can't survive without oxygen).

India grows a lot of fruit. It is the world's largest producer of bananas and grows half the world's mangoes.

Without bees we wouldn't have a third of the food we can eat, including apples, nuts and pumpkins. Bees spread pollen from plant to plant, which makes them grow.

Seeds from over 4,000 different plants are stored underground on a remote island in the Arctic Circle. If there was a disaster that destroyed our food crops, we'd be able to grow more.

The dye that makes sweets an attractive bright red colour is sometimes made from crushed beetles.

Seaweed is a common ingredient in ice cream. It helps the other ingredients to mix together.

Honey never goes bad if it's kept in a sealed jar. Honey in ancient Egyptian tombs could still be eaten today.

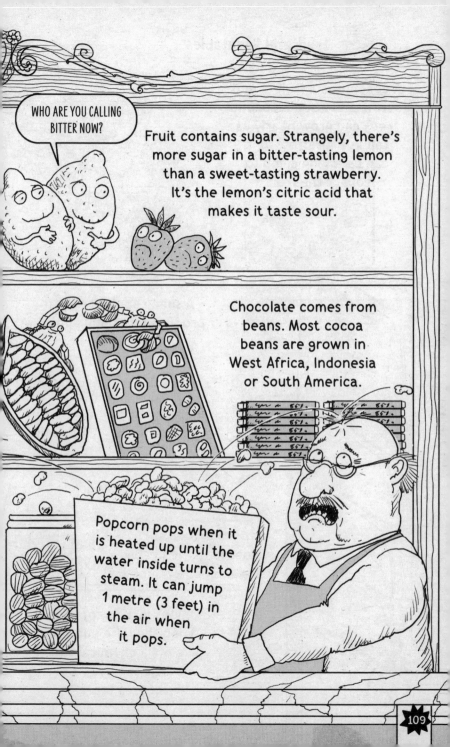

WHO ARE YOU CALLING BITTER NOW?

Fruit contains sugar. Strangely, there's more sugar in a bitter-tasting lemon than a sweet-tasting strawberry. It's the lemon's citric acid that makes it taste sour.

Chocolate comes from beans. Most cocoa beans are grown in West Africa, Indonesia or South America.

Popcorn pops when it is heated up until the water inside turns to steam. It can jump 1 metre (3 feet) in the air when it pops.

Fruit and Vegetables

A coconut is a fruit ... and a nut ... and a seed. Coconut trees can grow nearly as tall as 6 giraffes, so it can be a long climb to collect the fruit.

A single apple tree can produce up to 800 apples.

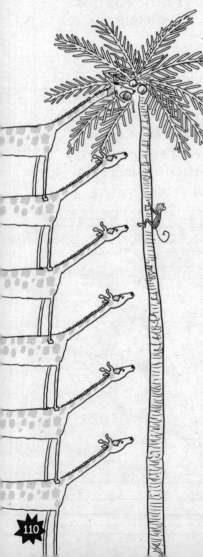

Onions make people cry. When they are cut, they give off a chemical which stings the eyes and causes tears.

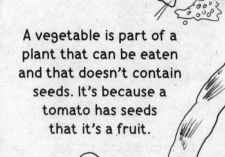

A vegetable is part of a plant that can be eaten and that doesn't contain seeds. It's because a tomato has seeds that it's a fruit.

Over 5 billion pizzas are sold worldwide every year. It's estimated that 350 slices are eaten in the USA every second.

The green juice from spinach leaves was used as an ink in medieval times.

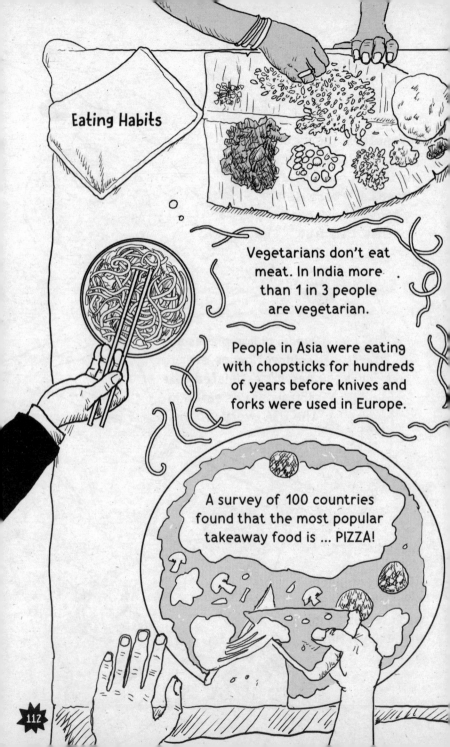

Eating Habits

Vegetarians don't eat meat. In India more than 1 in 3 people are vegetarian.

People in Asia were eating with chopsticks for hundreds of years before knives and forks were used in Europe.

A survey of 100 countries found that the most popular takeaway food is ... PIZZA!

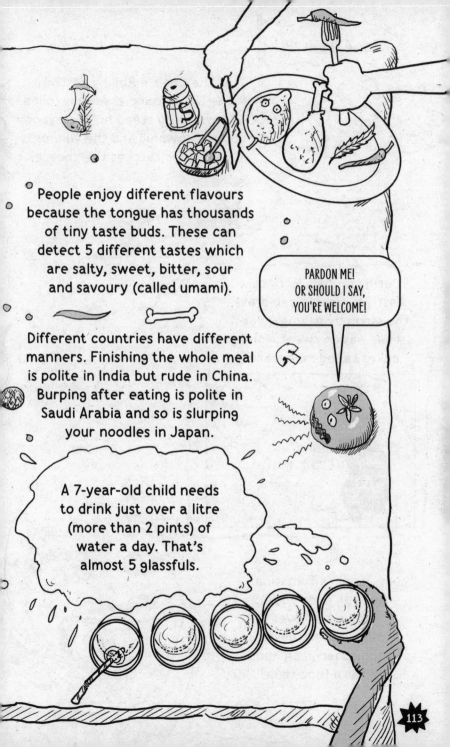

People enjoy different flavours because the tongue has thousands of tiny taste buds. These can detect 5 different tastes which are salty, sweet, bitter, sour and savoury (called umami).

Different countries have different manners. Finishing the whole meal is polite in India but rude in China. Burping after eating is polite in Saudi Arabia and so is slurping your noodles in Japan.

PARDON ME! OR SHOULD I SAY, YOU'RE WELCOME!

A 7-year-old child needs to drink just over a litre (more than 2 pints) of water a day. That's almost 5 glassfuls.

Food Festivals

At the Cheese Rolling Festival in the UK, a round cheese is rolled down a very steep hill. Everybody races downhill and the winner is whoever catches the cheese.

During China's Mooncake Festival, people celebrate the Moon by gazing up at it while eating sweet, round cakes called mooncakes.

At Spain's Tomatina festival, over 20,000 people hurl over a million tomatoes at each other in an hour. What a food fight!

CHAPTER 9:
SCIENCE

Plants

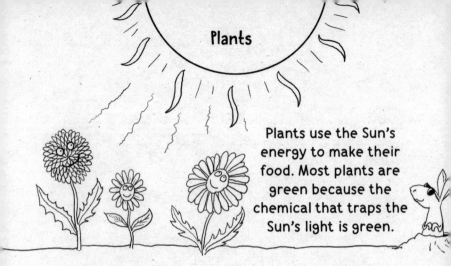

Plants use the Sun's energy to make their food. Most plants are green because the chemical that traps the Sun's light is green.

A saguaro cactus can hold enough water to fill 5 bathtubs right to the top. The water is no use to anyone lost in the desert, though, because it's full of nasty things and undrinkable.

OUCH! I JUST WANTED SOME WATER!

Plants have colourful petals to attract bees and other insects. These insects carry a powder (called pollen) from one flower to another which helps them to make more flowers.

The Rafflesia flower can grow so big it's almost as wide as a 7-year-old child's height. You won't see it in people's gardens because it smells of rotten meat!

Young sunflowers love the Sun so much that they follow it around. Their face will always look towards the Sun as it moves across the sky from east to west during the day.

Some tomato plants rely on a type of wasp to keep away a particular type of caterpillar. When the caterpillar starts to munch on the plant, the plant sends a chemical to attract wasps. The wasps then kill the caterpillar.

Food and Energy

Living creatures get energy from food and different animals need different amounts. A 7-year-old child needs 8 times more energy than a cat and 30 times less than an elephant.

Grass is eaten by grasshoppers. Grasshoppers are eaten by frogs. Frogs are eaten by snakes. Snakes are eaten by eagles. This is an example of a food chain.

The blue whale is the largest animal on Earth, but it eats tiny creatures called krill. Krill are only about 6 centimetres (2.4 inches) long, so a blue whale needs to eat around 4,000 kilograms (4 tonnes) of them a day.

I'M STARVING! I'VE ONLY EATEN 3 MILLION KRILL TODAY.

The egg-eating snake doesn't have any teeth, so it just swallows the whole egg. The egg isn't just larger than the snake's mouth. It's several times bigger than its entire head.

A bee has a sort of trunk like an elephant. It's called a proboscis and is used for sticking into flowers and drinking up the sweet-tasting juice called nectar.

Hummingbirds eat up to 3 times their own body weight in a day. That's like a 7-year-old child eating 600 quarter-pounder burgers in a day.

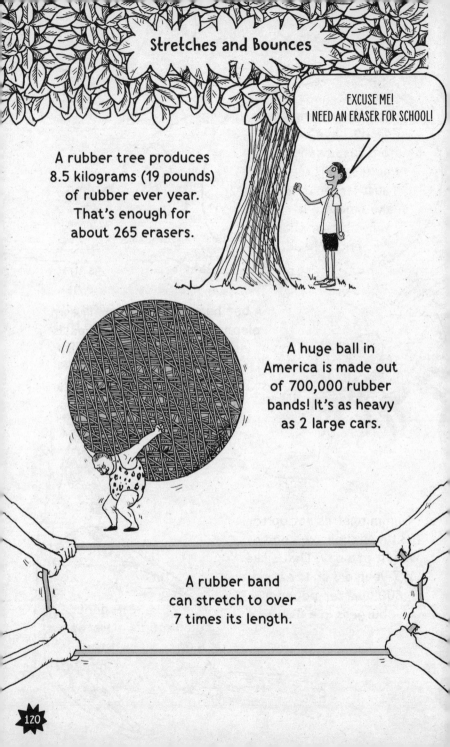

EXCUSE ME!
I NEED AN ERASER FOR SCHOOL!

A rubber tree produces 8.5 kilograms (19 pounds) of rubber ever year. That's enough for about 265 erasers.

A huge ball in America is made out of 700,000 rubber bands! It's as heavy as 2 large cars.

A rubber band can stretch to over 7 times its length.

Springs can make trampolines very bouncy. The highest-ever trampoline jump was higher than the height of a giraffe.

Slinkies are springs that stretch down to the next step, join together again and then stretch to the one below. The most steps a slinky has gone down without stopping is 30.

In 2014, a student completed a marathon on a pogo stick. It took him 16 hours and 24 minutes.

The Seasons

The seasons happen at different times around the world. Spring starts in March in the USA and Europe. It starts in September in Australia.

Norway is called the Land of the Midnight Sun because in summer the Sun doesn't set, so it's always daylight.

Autumn sees one of the world's most beautiful sights. Millions of bright, orange monarch butterflies fly hundreds of miles south from North America to find warmer weather.

Yakutsk in Russia is the world's coldest city. In winter, people can't wear spectacles outside because they freeze to their face.

THE RAINY SEASON CATCHES ME OUT EVERY YEAR.

Most countries have 4 seasons: spring, summer, autumn and winter. Some countries, such as Indonesia, only have 2: a dry season and a rainy season.

Water and Air

Ice is lighter than water
which is why ice floats.
Only some of an iceberg is
above the water, though.
In fact, 90% of an iceberg
is the bit you can't see.

About three-quarters
of a baby is water.

The metric system weighs
things in kilograms. For
example, 1 litre of water
weighs exactly 1 kilogram.

We breathe in enough air in 1 day to blow up over 600 balloons.

We need oxygen to live, but air is mostly made of a gas called nitrogen. There is almost 4 times more nitrogen than oxygen.

There is less oxygen on higher ground. At the top of Everest, climbers need 3 breaths to get the same amount of oxygen as 1 breath at the bottom. That's why they wear oxygen masks, like divers.

ER, I THINK YOU'VE TAKEN THIS A BIT FAR, MARIA.

125

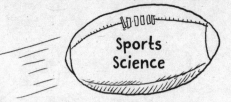

Sports Science

Adults walk about 5,000 steps on average every day, but children usually do at least twice as many.

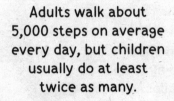

A person's heart rate can be 3 times faster when they exercise.

Running or skipping uses about 8 times more energy than sitting down.

Fauja Singh took up running when he was 81 years old. In 2011, he became the first 100-year-old to run a marathon, a distance of just over 42 kilometres (26 miles).

Dancing is a fantastic way to keep fit. Bandana Nepal might have overdone it a bit, though. She danced for over 5 days and nights ... non-stop.

Jordan Coen completed 14,657 rope-skips in an hour. That's just over 4 skips every second.

ALSO AVAILABLE:

ISBN: 978-1-78055-925-4   ISBN: 978-1-78055-927-8